CONTENTS

Some words are shown in bold, **like this**. You can find out what they mean by looking in the glossary.

WHO WERE THE VIKINGS?

Britain has been invaded many times in its history. In 55 BC, it was the Romans. In the AD 400s, the Anglo-Saxons arrived. Both groups eventually **settled** into their new home. But in AD 793, a new and terrifying group of invaders arrived: the Vikings. They **raided** towns and **monasteries**, killing and stealing before sailing back home.

Viking homelands

The Vikings came from what is now Denmark, Norway and Sweden. Around the late AD 700s, they began launching raids on other lands, such as Britain, France, Spain and Russia. Raiding helped the Vikings find wealth and land to farm. There may not have been enough good farming land to go round in their homelands. Places like Britain, where there were many small, weak kingdoms, were easy targets.

In 1016, a Viking called Cnut became king of England.

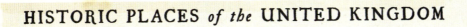

HISTORIC PLACES *of the* UNITED KINGDOM

VIKING
SITES

Nancy Dickmann

Raintree is an imprint of Capstone Global Library Limited, a company incorporated in England and Wales having its registered office at 264 Banbury Road, Oxford, OX2 7DY – Registered company number: 6695582

www.raintree.co.uk

myorders@raintree.co.uk

Text © Capstone Global Library Limited 2018

Produced for Raintree by

White-Thomson Publishing Ltd

+44 (0)1273 477 216

www.wtpub.co.uk

Edited by Nancy Dickmann
Designed by Clare Nicholas
Original illustrations © Capstone Global Library Ltd 2017
Illustrated by Ron Dixon
Production by Duncan Gilbert
Originated by Capstone Global Library Ltd
Printed and bound in India

ISBN 978 1 4747 5410 1 (hardcover)
21 20 19 18 17
10 9 8 7 6 5 4 3 2 1

ISBN 978 1 4747 5421 7 (paperback)
22 21 20 19 18
10 9 8 7 6 5 4 3 2 1

British Library Cataloguing in Publication Data
A full catalogue record for this book is available from the British Library.

Acknowledgements
We would like to thank the following for permission to reproduce photographs: Adam Stanford © Aerial-Cam Ltd., 9, 22 (detail), 24–25; Alamy: ART Collection, 28, Ashley Cooper, 16, Doug Houghton, 5, Doug Houghton Collection, 26, Heritage Image Partnership Ltd, 14, 21, imageBROKER, cover, 18, John Morrison, 22, Loop Images Ltd, 19; Courtesy of the Portable Antiquities Scheme, 3, 17 top (ID LIN-D3E540), 17 bottom, 31(ID NLM-7F954A); Getty Images: photos.com, 10, ManuelVelasco, 23; Courtesy of Manx National Heritage: 24;

... vi585, 11, GreenTree, 13, Michael Conrad, 8, 29, Peter ... 7, 15.

... the preparation for this book.

...ders of material reproduced in this book. Any omissions ...given to the publisher.

...were valid at the time of going to press. However, due to ... may have changed, or sites may have changed or ceased ...lisher regret any inconvenience this may cause readers, ...oted by either the author or the publisher.

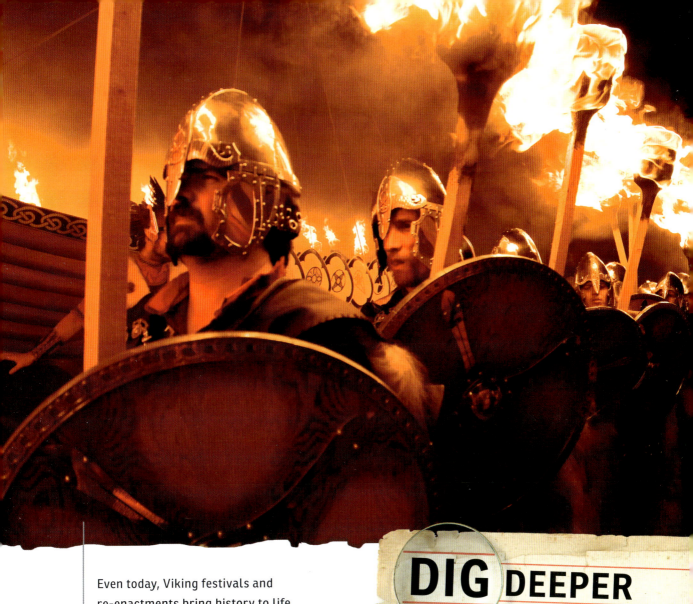

Even today, Viking festivals and re-enactments bring history to life.

Clash of cultures

The Vikings were part of a **Norse culture**. They were **pagans** who believed in many gods. The Anglo-Saxons who lived in Britain had originally been pagan too. By the time of the Viking invasion, though, they had mostly **converted** to Christianity. The two sides fought each other for centuries.

DIG DEEPER

** WHAT'S IN A NAME? **

Most Anglo-Saxons called the Vikings Danes or Norsemen, because of where they came from. *Viking* is a Norse word that can mean "going on a raid", or "raider". It may have come from an Old Norse word for *bay* because Viking raiders sailed out from bays in **Scandinavia**.

From raiders to settlers

At first, raiding in their fast, agile ships was all the Vikings did. They still had their homes in Scandinavia. In the AD 850s, some of the raiders started to spend the winters in Britain. They were beginning to settle permanently. A few years later, the Vikings began to assemble large armies. They were ready to take over the whole island.

Conquering Britain

Vikings from Norway settled in Orkney, and soon took over much of Scotland. In England, they slowly **conquered** the Anglo-Saxon kingdoms. Northumbria, East Anglia and Mercia all fell to the Vikings. By AD 874, only Wessex was left. Its king, Alfred the Great (AD 849–899), defeated the Vikings at the Battle of Edington in AD 878 and forced them back. The Vikings now ruled the eastern part of the island, and Alfred ruled the south and west.

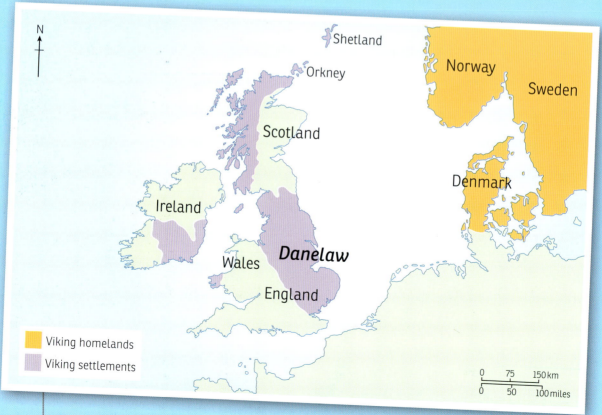

This map shows where Vikings settled in the British Isles.
The area of England ruled by the Vikings was later called the **Danelaw**.

Alfred the Great built fortified towns to help Wessex defend itself against the Vikings.

DIG DEEPER

** DANEGELD **

Sometimes people in Britain paid the Vikings so that they wouldn't be attacked. Starting in AD 991, English rulers began to collect a **tax** for just this purpose. It was later called Danegeld.

Lasting legacy

Vikings settled in large areas of Britain, and they married and mixed with the local population. They brought their art, language and customs with them. Few buildings are left from this time, but they left behind many **artefacts** that can still be seen today.

LINDISFARNE

Off the coast of northeast England stands the small island of Lindisfarne. It was once the site of a **monastery**, where Christian **monks** lived and worked. It was probably the first place in Britain to be **raided** by Vikings.

LINDISFARNE

A rich target

The monastery had been founded around AD 635 by an Irish monk called Aidan. By the time of the Viking raid in June AD 793, it was one of the holiest Christian sites in Britain. It would have had religious items made of gold and silver. It was also remote and unprotected, making it the perfect target.

WHAT: island site of a former monastery

WHERE: Northumberland coast

WHEN: AD 793

The castle on Lindisfarne was built in the 16th century. In AD 793, there was no fortress to protect against the Vikings.

Surprise attack

The Vikings arrived from the sea, sailing in fast ships. They took the monks by surprise, killing many of them. They also carried off most of the monastery's rich treasures. They were not interested in settling in Northumberland. They just took what they wanted, and then left. There would be more trouble soon to come.

DIG DEEPER

** VIKING SHIPS **

Viking ships were perfect for launching raids. These "**longships**" were built from overlapping planks of wood. They could be powered by oars or a sail. The ships were shallow enough to sail up rivers or even right onto a beach.

This stone was part of a grave marker. Its location may show where the original monastery on Lindisfarne stood.

Fear and panic

The people of Britain were terrified by the arrival of the Vikings. If the Vikings were willing to attack such a holy place, what else might they do? Although many of the monks on Lindisfarne had been killed, their community survived. However, they were worried about more raids. They finally left the island in AD 875.

DIG DEEPER

** ATTACK ON IONA **

The Scottish island of Iona, in the Inner Hebrides, was the site of another important monastery. The monastery was raided by Vikings in AD 795, then again in AD 802 and AD 806. After the third attack, most of the surviving monks fled to Ireland.

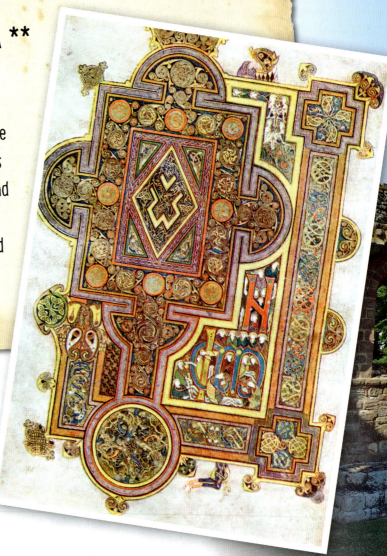

The monks on Iona were known for the beautifully illustrated books they produced, such as this one.

Only the beginning

What started on Lindisfarne soon became a pattern. Vikings raided other parts of the British Isles. They often targeted monasteries because their rich treasures were poorly defended. People never knew when the Vikings would arrive with their ships and swords. Then, in the AD 850s, they stopped going back home between raids. The Vikings were here to stay.

Viking leaders

Many stories from the time tell of a Viking king called Ragnar Lothbrok (whose name meant "hairy breeches"). He is said to have been killed by the king of Northumbria, and his son Ivarr wanted revenge. Ivarr and his brothers organized a huge Viking army to take over as much of Britain as they could.

In the early 1100s, Christian monks returned to Lindisfarne. They built a new **priory**, which can still be seen today.

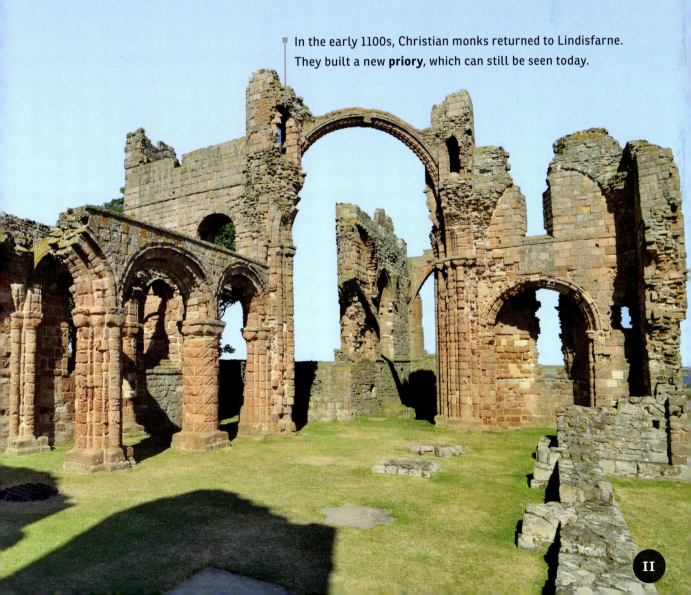

JORVIK

The city of York has a long and complicated history. It was founded around AD 71 by the Romans, who called it Eboracum. They made it an important city but left around AD 400. When the Anglo-Saxons arrived, they called it Eoforwic.

JORVIK

Viking capital

Two sons of Ragnar Lothbrok attacked Eoforwic in AD 866 and took full control the following spring. Many people were killed during the battle, including two Anglo-Saxon kings. The Vikings renamed the city Jorvik and soon **conquered** the land around the city. Jorvik became the capital of the **Danelaw**. From Jorvik, Viking kings ruled over large parts of the north and east of England.

WHAT: former Viking capital city

WHERE: York

WHEN: from AD 867-954

York is still an important city, but none of the Viking buildings is still there.

DIG DEEPER

** DISTANT CONNECTIONS **

Some of the items found at Jorvik tell us where the Vikings traded. **Archaeologists** digging there found a coin from the area that is now Uzbekistan. They have also found **amber** that probably came from the coast of the Baltic Sea.

Trading network

Jorvik became a hub for trade. Traders there probably did business with people from all over Britain, as well as much farther away. Vikings traded for exotic goods, such as silk, amber and spices. Many of these goods came through Jorvik before being sold on.

In the past, cowrie shells were often used as money. A cowrie shell from the Red Sea was found at Jorvik.

Manufacturing

Craft workers in Jorvik made goods that were sold throughout the Danelaw and beyond. **Raw materials**, such as copper, tin, ivory, lead and wool came from many kilometres away. Skilled workers produced clay pots, knives, keys, jewellery, combs and clothing. These products could be sold locally or taken abroad by traders.

The Vikings at Jorvik made silver coins for buying and selling goods.

Busy city

From 1976–1981, archaeologists explored a site in central York. They found the remains of Viking buildings, as well as more than 40,000 **artefacts**. These finds tell the story of the people who lived and worked in Jorvik. Their homes and workshops were made from wood and **thatch** and were built very close together. Ships were constantly arriving and leaving from the port on the River Ouse.

Forced out

Life in Viking Jorvik continued for nearly a century. In 947, a man called Eirik Bloodaxe became king. After a series of battles with the armies of the English king, Eadred, Eirik was forced out of Jorvik. After that, York and Northumbria became part of a united England. However, although York was now ruled by an English king, it kept its Viking **culture**.

Several **hoards** of Viking silver have been found. These objects would have been very valuable, showing the wealth of some of Britain's Vikings.

DIG DEEPER

** VIKING ECHOES **

Traces of York's Viking history can still be seen today. Many modern streets have names ending in "gate", such as Micklegate and Skeldergate. They come from the Viking word *gata*, which means "street".

15

GOSFORTH STONE CROSS

GOSFORTH

WHAT: stone cross

WHERE: Gosforth, Cumbria

WHEN: between AD 900 and 950

When the Vikings arrived, many of the people in Britain were Christians. The Vikings were not – they were **pagans** who believed in many gods. But once they **settled**, they began to **convert** to Christianity. The stone cross in Gosforth is a symbol of this change.

Viking beliefs

Historians don't know much about how the Vikings originally worshipped. They may have gathered in temples or at sacred trees. They may have **sacrificed** animals – or even humans – to their gods. They told many stories about gods and monsters. These **myths** have survived and are still popular.

The Gosforth stone cross stands 4.4 metres (14 feet) high.

DIG DEEPER

** PAGAN GODS **

Odin was the ruler of the **Norse** gods. Loki was a trickster who often caused trouble. Fierce Thor, with his magical hammer, was the god of thunder. Vikings often wore **amulets** in the shape of Thor's hammer. They believed these lucky charms would protect them.

Converting to Christianity

Becoming Christians may have been a way for Vikings to make peace with their new Christian neighbours. Many Vikings also married Christians. Christianity soon became the main religion for Vikings in Britain. The stone cross at Gosforth shows the mix of **cultures**. A cross is a Christian symbol, but the carvings on it show figures from Norse myths.

Thor's hammer amulet

This silver pendant shows the Norse god Odin.

SHETLAND

SHETLAND

The Shetland Islands were under Viking control longer than almost any other part of Britain. It was only in the late 1400s that their Viking rulers passed the islands back to Scotland. Viking **culture** lives on in Shetland, and the remains of many Viking buildings have been found there.

History of Shetland

When the Vikings arrived in around AD 800, the people living in Shetland belonged to a tribe called the Picts. The Vikings took over and used Shetland as a base for launching **raids** on Norway and the Scottish mainland. For many years, Shetland was part of the earldom of Orkney, belonging to the Kingdom of Norway.

WHAT: islands formerly under Viking control

WHERE: north of the Scottish mainland

WHEN: about AD 800-1468

This longhouse on the island of Unst once had an upper and a lower room.

Living in Shetland

Vikings lived and farmed in Shetland for hundreds of years. **Archaeologists** have found the remains of more than 60 homes. They have also found **quarries**, where Vikings collected a mineral called soapstone. They made it into cooking pots and other items that could be traded. There was also a local *thing*, or parliament, where officials made laws and tried criminals.

DIG DEEPER

** VIKING HOUSES **

Viking families lived in buildings called longhouses. Many longhouses in Shetland were built of wood with an outer "skin" of stone. Roofs may have had a layer of turf on the top. A longhouse had a central hearth for cooking and warmth.

Archaeologists have built a replica of a Viking longhouse on Unst.

Farming and food

Vikings had a reputation as fierce raiders, but many of them were actually simple farmers. On farms like the ones in Shetland, they grew oats, barley and vegetables. They raised pigs and cows, as well as sheep, goats and chickens. Vikings used the animals for meat and made milk into cheese and butter. They could preserve meat and fish by smoking or drying it.

Viking families

Some Viking men came over as raiders. Once they had won a piece of land, they could bring their families over to join them. They **settled** as farmers but could still be called on to fight if needed. Viking women worked hard weaving cloth, milking cows, cooking and looking after the children. The children didn't go to school. Instead, they helped their parents and learned important skills.

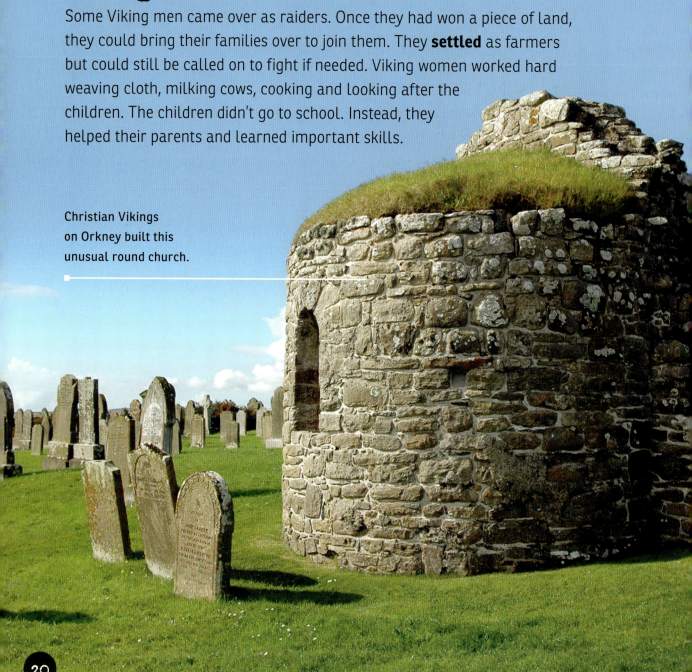

Christian Vikings
on Orkney built this
unusual round church.

DIG DEEPER

** NORN **

The Orkney Islands were also settled by Vikings from Norway. In Orkney and Shetland, the Vikings spoke a version of the **Norse** language called Norn. This language was never written down, and it died out in the 19th century.

Entertainment

Viking settlers worked hard, but they also made time to have fun. Men took part in wrestling contests or other sports. People also played board games to pass the time. In the evenings, Vikings would sometimes gather in a longhouse to listen to songs and stories about legendary heroes.

Some Vikings used pieces like these when playing board games.

HEYSHAM HOGBACK STONE

St Peter's Church stands in the Lancashire village of Heysham. Inside it is an unusual carved stone. It is called a **hogback** stone, but it has nothing to do with pigs. Instead, it was used as a marker on a Viking grave.

HEYSHAM

Hogback stones

Similar stones have been found elsewhere in Britain, but not in Denmark or Norway. They are found throughout the region that formed the **Danelaw**. Hogback stones were placed over graves, and they were carved to look like Viking homes. Some of them had fierce beasts carved at the ends.

WHAT: carved gravestone
WHERE: Heysham, Lancashire
WHEN: around AD 1000

Archaeologists can't agree on what all the carvings on the Heysham stone represent.

Many people think this figure is the **Norse** hero Sigurd.

Carvings

The Heysham hogback stone has carvings along the top that represent a tiled roof. On one side, this roof is supported by four human figures. There are also carvings of creatures from Norse **myths**. These myths date back to the Vikings' **pagan** days. However, the stone was found in a churchyard, so the person buried beneath it may have been a Christian.

DIG DEEPER

** THE VIKING AFTERLIFE **

Before they **converted** to Christianity, Vikings had different ideas about the afterlife. They believed that brave warriors would go to Valhalla when they died. This was a grand hall where there would be feasting and fighting. Vikings were buried with things that they might need in the afterlife.

Many Vikings were **cremated** instead of being buried. They believed the smoke would carry them away to the afterlife.

BALLADOOLE SHIP BURIAL

Near the southern tip of the Isle of Man, two rows of stones are arranged in the shape of a boat. They mark the site of a fantastic discovery: the remains of a Viking man, buried on his ship with all his belongings around him.

BALLADOOLE

Trading boat

Boats were very important to the Vikings, and they sometimes buried people in them. The boat at Balladoole was about 12 metres (40 feet) long. It was probably the type of ship that traders used to carry cargo. **Artefacts** found in the ship came from different places in Britain and Ireland. They show that the Isle of Man was an important stop for traders.

WHAT: ship burial

WHERE: near Castletown, Isle of Man

WHEN: around AD 950

The ship burial was discovered and **excavated** in 1945.

DIG DEEPER

** THE TYNWALD **

Today, the Isle of Man parliament is called the Tynwald. Its name comes from the **Norse** word *thing*. Once a year, it meets outdoors on Tynwald Hill, and new laws are read out. This is a ceremony that dates back to Viking times.

Who was it?

The man buried in the ship was probably rich and important. He was buried fully clothed with a knife and a shield. Animal bones were found above the burial, showing that livestock might have been burned as a **sacrifice**. Ordinary people wouldn't have had such a complicated burial.

The wooden ship had rotted away, but this model shows what it would have looked like when it was buried.

VIKING NAMES

The Vikings didn't leave behind grand palaces or castles.
However, their memory lives on thanks to their language.
Many of the words in modern English are based on **Norse** words.
There are also traces of the Norse language in the names of places.

Loan words

When the Vikings **settled** in Britain, they brought their
language with them. Many of their words are still in use
today. Words like *berserk*, *club*, and *ransack* all come from
Norse – not surprising given the Vikings' reputation as fierce
warriors. But we also get everyday words such as *husband*,
bug, *cake*, *dirt*, *stain* and *sky* from the Vikings.

The Viking language
was written down
using shapes
called runes. These
carved runes were
found in Orkney.

Viking places

Viking place names are made up of smaller words. They describe a place's setting or its purpose. Here are just a few of them:

Word	Meaning	Example
by	farm or village	Derby
dale	valley	Colsterdale
holm	islet or raised ground	Burthholme
kirk	church	Romaldkirk
thorpe	farm	Scunthorpe
toft	site of a house	Lowestoft

DIG DEEPER

** ACTIVITY **

If you live in Ireland or the north or east of Britain, take a look at a map of your local area. Can you find any villages, towns or cities that have Viking names? Do they match up with the natural features in their meanings, such as valleys? If you live in a different part of the country, try to spot the Viking names in other areas.

Derby's name has Viking origins. It means "village of the deer".

THE END OF THE VIKINGS

In the AD 900s, the English took back a lot of the land that the Vikings had **conquered**. Eirik Bloodaxe, the last Viking king of Jorvik, was defeated in AD 954. In 1016, the Viking King Cnut made England part of his empire, but Viking rule in Britain would soon be over for good.

Norman invasion

In 1066, an army from Normandy, France, invaded England. The **Normans** were actually the descendants of Vikings who had **settled** in France! They were commanded by William the Conqueror, who took over all of England. Vikings remained in control of part of Scotland, but this came to an end in 1468, when Shetland and Orkney became part of Scotland.

The last major Viking invasion of Britain took place in 1066 at the Battle of Stamford Bridge.

Timeline

AD 793	Viking raiders attack the holy island of Lindisfarne.
AD 795	Viking raiders attack the **monastery** at Iona for the first time.
around AD 800	Vikings arrive in Shetland.
AD 865	The Vikings assemble a large army to conquer England.
AD 867	Vikings establish a kingdom centred in Jorvik (York).
AD 869	King Edmund of East Anglia is killed by Vikings.
AD 871	Alfred the Great becomes king of Wessex.
AD 878	Alfred's army defeats the Viking army at the Battle of Edington.
around AD 886	Alfred signs an agreement with the Viking king Guthrum, dividing England into Anglo-Saxon lands and the **Danelaw**.
AD 900–950	A stone cross is erected in Gosforth, Cumbria.
around AD 950	An important Viking is buried in a ship at Balladoole on the Isle of Man.
AD 954	The Viking king Eirik Bloodaxe is driven out of Jorvik.
AD 991	The English king Æthelred pays the first Danegeld to prevent Viking attacks.
around 1000	A Viking is buried in Heysham with a **hogback** stone over his grave.
1013	Vikings from Denmark reconquer England.
1016	Cnut becomes king of England.
1066	The Saxon king Harold defeats a Viking invasion at the Battle of Stamford Bridge.
	William the Conqueror wins the Battle of Hastings and takes over England.
1266	Norway gives the Outer Hebrides and the Isle of Man to Scotland.
1468	Orkney and Shetland become part of Scotland.

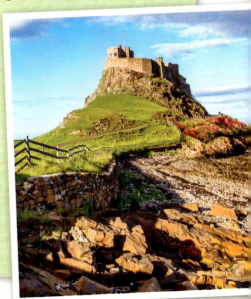

Glossary

amber yellowish-brown substance formed from fossilized tree sap

amulet small charm believed to protect the wearer from harm

archaeologist person who learns about the past by digging up old buildings or objects and studying them

artefact object used in the past that was made by people

conquer defeat and take control of an enemy

convert persuade someone to follow a different religion

cremate burn to ashes. Human bodies are often cremated.

culture group of people's way of life, ideas, art, customs and traditions

Danelaw area of northern and eastern England where Vikings had control

excavate dig in the earth

hoard money or other valuables that are stored, buried or hidden away

hogback long carved stone placed over the graves of some Vikings

longship simple wooden ship used by the Vikings. Longships were fast and easy to steer.

monastery building where monks live

monk man in a religious community who has vowed to live simply

myth story from ancient times

Norman member of a group of people with Scandinavian ancestry who moved to northern France in the AD 900s

Norse having to do with the people or languages of ancient Scandinavia

pagan person who worships many gods instead of just one

priory religious house

quarry place where stone is dug out of the ground

raid sudden, surprise attack on a place

raw material natural substances that are processed and used to make goods

sacrifice offer something to a god

Scandinavia part of northern Europe that includes Norway, Denmark and Sweden

settle make a home in a new place

tax money collected from a country's people which is paid to its rulers

thatch covering for houses made of straw or grass

thing old Norse word for a parliament

Find out more

BOOKS

The Anglo-Saxons and Vikings (History of Britain), Hazel Maskell and Abigail Wheatley (Usborne Publishing, 2015)

Ivar the Boneless and the Vikings (History Starting Points), David Gill (Franklin Watts, 2016)

Vikings (Britain in the Past), Moira Butterfield (Franklin Watts, 2015)

Vikings (Explore!), Jane Bingham (Wayland, 2015)

Vikings (Fact Cat: History: Early Britons), Izzi Howell (Wayland, 2015)

WEBSITES

www.bbc.co.uk/education/topics/ztyr9j6
Go here to find learning guides about the Vikings.

www.dkfindout.com/uk/history/vikings/
This site is chock-full of facts about Vikings.

www.jorvikvikingcentre.co.uk
The website of the Jorvik Viking Centre tells all about the history of the Vikings in Jorvik (York).

www.natgeokids.com/uk/discover/history/general-history/10-facts-about-the-vikings/
Learn some awesome Viking facts on this website.

PLACES TO VISIT

Balladoole
(Viking ship burial)
Castletown, Isle of Man, IM9 4PQ

The British Museum
(home of many Viking artefacts)
London, WC1B 3DG

The Dock Museum
(home of Viking artefacts)
Barrow-in-Furness, Cumbria, LA14 2PW

Jarlshof
(former Viking settlement)
Sumburgh, Shetland, ZE3 9JN

Jorvik Viking Centre
(museum about Viking life)
York, North Yorkshire, YO1 9WT

Lindisfarne
(site of Viking raid)
Holy Island, Northumberland, TD15 2RX

St Mary's Church
(site of Gosforth stone cross)
Gosforth, Cumbria, CA20 1AU

St Peter's Church
(site of hogback stone)
Heysham, Lancashire, LA3 2RN

Viking Experience
(interactive exhibit about Vikings)
Largs, Ayrshire, KA30 8QL

Index